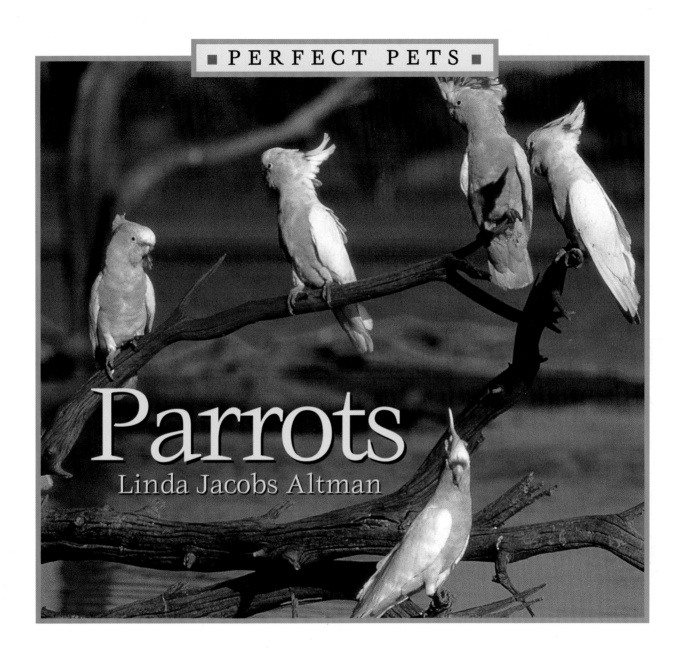

■ PERFECT PETS ■

# Parrots

## Linda Jacobs Altman

# BENCHMARK BOOKS

MARSHALL CAVENDISH

NEW YORK

Benchmark Books
Marshall Cavendish Corporation
99 White Plains Road
Tarrytown, New York 10591

Library of Congress Cataloging-in-Publication Data
Altman, Linda Jacobs, date.
Parrots/Linda Jacobs Altman.
p.   cm. — (Perfect Pets)
Includes bibliographical references.
Summary: Provides information about the history, physical
characteristics, choosing, and care of all kinds of parrots.
ISBN 0-7614-1102-X (lib. bdg.)
1. Parrots—Juvenile literature. [1. Parrots.  2. Pets.]  I. Title.
II. Series.
SF473.P3.A47    2001    636.6'865 dc21    99-049672    CIP    AC

Photo research by Candlepants, Inc.

Cover photo: *Photo Researchers, Inc*: Sylvain Grandadam
Back cover photo: *Animals Animals*: Renee Stockdale

The photographs in this book are used by permission and
through the courtesy of: *Animals Animals*: Klaus Uhlenhut,
title page; Fritz Prenzel, 3; Gerard Lacz, 13 (left) Tilford. T, 13
(right); J & P Wegner, 18, 28; Michael Dick, 21; Renee Stockdale,
23, 24; Robert Maier, 25. *Art Resource*, NY: Scala, 6; Erich Lessing,
7, 29. *Dennis Sheridan*: 11, 12, 14, 16, 30. *Photo Researchers, Inc.*:
George Holton, 4; Andy Levin, 9; Francois Gohier, 10; T.
McHugh, 17, 22; Kenneth Fink, 19; Tony Hamblin, 20; David M.
Grossman, 26 (top); Larry Mulvehill, 26 (bottom); Margaret
Miller, 27.

Printed in Hong Kong
6    5    4    3    2

*For Worf and Troi,
the only cockatiels in Star Fleet.*

*The scarlet macaw is one of the most colorful birds in the world.*

# Parrots

make great pets. They are friendly, funny, and clever. They often amaze people with the things they can do. Parrots come in all sizes, from the tiny pygmy to the big macaw. The pygmy could fit on the short edge of a postcard. The macaw would need a yardstick and then some.

These amazing birds are natural mimics. They copy sounds. They can chime like doorbells, scream like sirens, or even bark like dogs. With careful teaching, many of them can learn to talk.

One of the first written descriptions of parrots comes from ancient Greece, nearly three thousand years ago. The writer described a plum-headed parakeet and noted that it could talk.

*Parrots captured the fancy of many artists. This Roman mosaic shows two parrots and a dove drinking from a fountain.*

Christopher Columbus discovered New World parrots on his famous voyage of 1492. He captured several and took them back to Europe, where they soon became popular pets.

This was probably the beginning of the long friendship between sailors and parrots. In those days, life at sea was hard. So were the men who lived that life. Sailors were known for rough manners and equally rough language.

Their parrots became famous for the same things. Aboard ship, the intelligent birds picked up a mixture of sailing terms, swear words, and rude noises.

The sailors loved it. Respectable folk didn't like it at all. Anyone who bought a sailor's parrot was in for a shock. No matter how hard the new owners tried, their pets never forgot how to "cuss like a sailor."

*After Columbus's famous voyage, parrots were in demand as pets. Sailors took them back from the New World and sold them at high prices. Here, a sixteenth-century lady shows off her parrot.*

*In* Treasure Island *by Robert Louis Stevenson, the pirate Long John Silver kept a pet parrot. Illustrations for the book often show the parrot perched on Long John's shoulder. This one is by the artist N. C. Wyeth.*

# Pirates and Parrots

Parrots and pirates seem to go together. In story and legend, every self-respecting pirate had certain things. He had a three-cornered hat on his head, a patch over one eye, and a parrot on his shoulder.

Today, a group called Pirates and Parrots brings these legends to life. The "pirates" are expert bird trainers. They dress in costume and put on shows. Twelve large parrots travel with them. The parrots talk and do tricks. They also let people pet them.

The shows are a lot of fun, but they also have a serious purpose. In the wild, many parrot species are endangered. The pirates work with a group that is trying to save them. Their shows help people understand why it is important to protect these beautiful birds.

*Parrots and pirates have a long history together. This parrot is dressed for the part.*

*Green-winged macaws in the wild. The cliffs are their home.*

# Columbus's

parrots were amazons. This **species** is still popular with bird lovers. Amazons are known as good talkers. Like most parrots, they are also known as good screechers. Sailors used to call them *kriken* (kREE-kin). This comes from the French word for "screech."

Other popular large parrots are the macaw, the African grey, and the cockatoo. All of them are beautiful. All of them can be noisy, messy, and demanding. They can also be charming and affectionate.

Macaws are big, colorful birds. The blue-gold macaw is bright blue, light blue, emerald green, and yellow. The scarlet macaw is bright red, with

*African grey parrots are excellent talkers. This one is named Nelson Mandela, in honor of the South African leader.*

*The sulphur crested cockatoo is powdery white, with a soft yellow crest and undertail. Adults are about twenty inches (fifty centimeters) long.*

yellow and blue. Macaws learn tricks easily. This makes them favorites in performing bird shows and in movies.

African greys are not as colorful as macaws. Their color is a soft dove gray, with streaks of red on the tail. They are known as the best talkers of all the parrots. Their speaking voices sound almost human.

Cockatoos are white, pink, or black. They have crests of upright feathers on their heads. Cockatoos are natural acrobats—beautiful showoffs who love an audience. An average size for cockatoos is about twenty inches (fifty centimeters). They are just a little shorter than an unfolded newspaper.

Their smaller cousins, the cockatiels, are less than half

Lovebirds are among the smallest of the parrots. These Fischer's lovebirds have featherless rings around their eyes.

The lesser sulphur crested cockatoo measures about fourteen inches (thirty-five centimeters).

The little lorikeet is a delightful explosion of color. It is native to Australia.

that size. Cockatiels, parakeets, and lovebirds are the most popular of the small parrots. Although they may be small, they are quite sturdy and fearless. Many of them can even talk and do tricks.

Cockatiels are usually gray with touches of white, orange, and yellow. Like the cockatoos, they have beautiful crests on their heads.

Parakeets and lovebirds are smaller yet. The normal color for a parakeet is green, with yellow, black, and white. There are several species of lovebirds. The best-known is the peach-faced lovebird. It is light green, with a face the color of sunrise and white rings around its eyes.

# Alex the African Grey

Alex is a most unusual parrot. He can name more than one hundred objects. He can talk about their color, shape, and size. He can even count up to six.

Alex doesn't just rattle off numbers. He knows what the numbers mean. For example, a trainer showed Alex two keys of different colors. When the trainer asked what they were, Alex said "keys." When the trainer asked how many, Alex said "two."

"What's different?" asked the trainer.

"Color," said the intelligent bird.

*Macaws can crack nuts with their powerful beaks. These two friends are playing.*

# Parrots

have large heads with strong, hooked beaks. Both the top and bottom parts of the beak move up and down. This comes in handy for cracking nuts or seeds. It is also good for climbing. Parrots are skilled at grabbing things with their beaks.

The foot of a parrot has four toes. Two point forward and two backward. This allows parrots to use their feet almost like hands. Parrots are forever picking up things with their feet—food, toys, sticks, pencils. Anything small enough to grasp is fair game.

Parrots are sociable birds. In the wild, they live together in **flocks**. When they mate, it is for life. The bond between mates is strong. Parrots have been known to die shortly after the loss of a partner.

*Parrots can learn to do many tricks. Here, a hyacinth macaw shows off for the camera.*

At nesting time, the partners find a cozy hollow in an old tree. The female lays about three to five eggs at a time. The babies hatch in three to four weeks. In most species, both parents help care for the **hatchlings**.

Sight is the most important sense to parrots. They can see better than humans, but they cannot use both eyes together. This is because their eyes are on either side of the head. To look at something directly in front, they must turn their head.

Above: *At four weeks, these baby parakeets have most of their feathers.*

Opposite: *Parrots enjoy preening, or grooming, one another. It not only keeps them clean; it is an act of friendship.*

*Good breeders keep their birds in large, comfortable aviaries. There is room to perch and even room to fly in this parakeet aviary.*

Parrots communicate with sound and action. They shriek or chatter for attention. They strut and flare their feathers to show off. They stretch their neck and hiss when they're angry. In the wild, they use special calls to communicate with other members of the flock.

Scientists aren't sure how long wild parrots live. Parrots in captivity have long life spans. Macaws, cockatoos, and amazons can live for a hundred years or more. Lovebirds and cockatiels sometimes live nearly thirty years.

# Those Wonderful Feathers

A bird's **plumage** does a lot more than just make it pretty. Wing and tail feathers help the bird to fly. Soft, inner feathers called down protect it from heat and cold. Harder outer feathers protect it from rain. Water slides right off the bird's back.

The coloring of feathers lets the bird blend into its surroundings. This helps it hide from enemies. A bird's coloring suits its environment. This is why most parrots are brightly colored. They come from rain forests and jungles, where they "disappear" into the colors of tropical fruits and flowers.

*A parrot spreads its wings, showing "flight feathers."*

*Parrots need roomy cages. Many owners also have stands, where the bird can sit outside its cage during the day.*

# The best place

to buy a parrot is from a **breeder** who hand-tames his or her birds. The babies are taken from the nest when they are about two weeks old. Humans feed them, using droppers and spoons. These babies grow up feeling comfortable with people. That makes them affectionate and easy to tame.

Choose a bird with sleek feathers and bright eyes. It should be alert and active. It is a good idea to have a **veterinarian** check the bird to be sure there are no problems.

Your bird will need a cage. Buy the biggest, sturdiest one you can afford. Of course, "big" means one thing for a parakeet and another for a macaw. The breeder or pet shop will

*A veterinarian prepares to examine two of his feathered patients.*

know what sizes are best. Be sure the bird has room to spread its wings and move around.

The cage should be furnished with perches, swings, and perhaps a climbing ladder or "tree." Parrots are messy eaters. They scatter seed husks everywhere. This means that cleaning is a daily job. Clean and refill the food and water dishes. Clean the cage and put fresh paper on the floor.

Parrots are seed-eaters, but seeds alone are not enough. They also need vegetables, fruits, grains, and minerals. There should always be **mineral blocks** and **cuttlebones** in the cage. The bird will also need gravel to help it digest its food.

Regular grooming is also important. Most parrots love to bathe. Give your bird a little tub of water, and it will do the rest. Parrots also need regular wing clipping and nail trimming. Pet shops often have people who can do this work. If not, ask your veterinarian.

*Parakeets love playgrounds with lots of ladders, perches, swings, and toys.*

When your parrot has adjusted to its new home, begin taming it. Start with a perch or an ordinary stick. Rub the stick gently against the bird's body, just above the legs. Say "Up!" Speak softly, and move slowly. The bird will probably flap its wings, squawk, and try to get away. Be patient. Keep repeating the word and the action.

*Hanging seed treats add variety to a bird's diet.*

# Dangerous Things

Many things that are safe for other pets can be harmful to birds. Ordinary things like aerosol sprays and scented candles can make birds sick. Nonstick coatings on pots and pans, grills, and many other objects are especially dangerous.

If these coatings get too hot, they give off fumes that can kill birds. Many bird owners get rid of all their coated utensils and appliances. If this is impossible, keep birds away from the kitchen. Don't let coated cookware get too hot. A smoking skillet can mean more than a burned dinner. It can mean a dead bird.

When the bird learns to climb on the stick, begin teaching it to climb onto your hand. Offer your finger to a small parrot, your hand or wrist to a larger one. Work the same way as before.

Soon your pet will be climbing onto your arm, your shoulder, and even your head. It will be affectionate and playful. If you want it to talk, this is the time to start.

Teaching a parrot to talk takes a

*Parrots are naturally sociable birds. Properly trained, they accept "their" humans as part of the flock.*

*Toddlers should learn to play with their parrots without grabbing or squeezing.*

lot of patience. Some birds will learn quickly, and some will learn slowly. Some may not learn at all. Start with a short word. Many owners use "hello."

Take the bird on your hand, and say the word over and over. Nuzzle the bird, and let it nuzzle you. Keep the sessions friendly, and keep them short. Short sessions are better than longer ones.

The first word may seem to take forever. Other words come faster. Many parrots will begin picking up new words on their own. This can lead to some hilarious surprises. One macaw learned to say, "I already did my homework!" An amazon who belonged to a football fan learned to yell, "Touchdown!"

Expect surprises like this when a parrot comes into your life. Expect a lot of work and a lot of fun. Expect some noise and confusion. Owning a parrot will bring all these things, and most owners wouldn't have it any other way.

*Parrots are fun to watch. A forked branch, a spray of millet seed, and a healthy parakeet can be more fun than television.*

# The Shivering Parrots

*A Story From India*

Long ago, there was a rich merchant who owned a parrot. Once when the merchant was going on a trip, the parrot asked him for a favor.

"When you pass through the forest where I was born, say hello to my friends. Tell them I have lived with you for many years. Tell them I have a cage of my very own."

"I will do as you ask," said the merchant and went on his way.

When he got to the forest, he found the parrot's friends and gave them the message. Upon hearing his words, all the parrots shivered and fell dead at his feet. The merchant was horrified.

When he got home, he told his parrot the terrible news.

Upon hearing it, the merchant's parrot also shivered and fell dead.

*In this seventeenth-century painting, a macaw adds color to an already colorful scene.*

Once more, the merchant was horrified. He opened the cage door to take out the parrot and bury it. When he did this, the parrot flapped its wings and flew past the startled merchant.

"My friends didn't really die," said the parrot. "They were telling me how I could escape. So I pretended to die as they did, and now I am free."

With that, the parrot flew out the window, and the merchant never saw it again.

# Fun Facts

Birds have an inner eyelid that moves across the eye like a windshield wiper.

Birds cannot move their eyeballs.

There are about 350 kinds of parrots.

One blue-fronted amazon lived to be 117 years old.

The oldest parrot fossil ever found was 40 to 50 million years old.

The kakapo parrot of New Zealand is the only flightless parrot in the world.

In 1890, the Zoological (animal study) Society of London said that parrots do not drink water. They were wrong, of course.

# Glossary

**breeder:** A person who raises animals, usually for sale.

**cuttlebone:** The inner shell of the cuttlefish. Used to give caged birds needed calcium.

**flock:** A group of birds of the same kind that live together.

**hatchling:** A newborn bird.

**mineral block:** A pressed cake of several minerals.

**plumage:** A bird's covering of feathers.

**species:** A group of animals or plants that share common traits.

**veterinarian:** A doctor who cares for animals.

# Find Out More About Parrots

Benitez, Mirna and Yvette Banek. *Super Parrot.* Austin, TX: Raintree/Steck Vaughn Publishers. 1990.

Heller, Ruth. *How to Hide a Parakeet & Other Birds.* New York: Grosset & Dunlap. 1995.

Martin, Rafe and Bethanne Andersen. *The Brave Little Parrot.* New York: Putnam Publishing Group. 1998.

Serventy, Vincent. *Parrot: Animals in the Wild.* Austin, TX: Raintree/Steck-Vaughn Publishers. 1998.

*The Pet Bird Report:* www.petbirdreport.com

# Index

African grey  11, 15
Amazon  11, 20, 30

beak  16, 17
body language  20
breeder  20, 23

cages  22, 24, 25, 29
cockatiel  12, 15, 20
cockatoo  12, 13, 15, 20
Columbus  5, 7

diet  24

feathers  18, 20, 21, 23

grooming  18, 19, 24

hatchling  18, 23
health  21, 24

lovebird  13, 15, 20

macaw  4, 5, 10-12, 16, 17, 20
mineral block  24

pirate  7-9

training  25-27

veterinarian  23

# About the Author

Linda Jacobs Altman has written many books for young people, including *Small Dogs* and *Big Dogs* in the Benchmark *Perfect Pets* series. She and her husband live in northern California with four dogs, four cats, and two cockatiels.